"CODEQUEST: A KID'S ADVENTURE IN PYTHON"

Contents

4

The Purpose of Python for Kids: An Introduction

Python is a phenomenal language for youngsters to begin their coding process. The following are some of the advantages of learning Python:

Simple to Write and Read: Python's linguistic structure is intended to be straightforward and clear, settling on it a fantastic decision for novices.

Versatile: Python is utilized in different fields, from web advancement to information science. Learning Python opens up a universe of opportunities for future undertakings.

Significant Community Support: There is a large and active Python community. This implies there are a lot of assets and backing accessible on the web.

Incredible for Critical thinking: Kids are able to concentrate on problem-solving and creative expression thanks to Python's straightforward syntax.

1.2 Creating a Python Environment for Kids efore beginning coding, a Python environment must be created. A guide that goes through each step:

Introduce Python:

Check out python.org.
Go to the "Downloads" segment and pick the most recent rendition appropriate for your working framework (Windows, macOS, or Linux).
Follow the steps for installation.
IDE (Incorporated Improvement Climate):

For novices, utilizing an IDE like Inactive, Thonny, or Jupyter Journal can be useful.
The coding process is made easier thanks to these environments' user-friendly interfaces.

To all of you:

Open the Python IDE after the installation.

Compose a basic program that prints "Hi, World!" to guarantee the setup's success.

1.3 The Basics of Python Syntax

Now that the environment is set up, let's look at some of the fundamentals of Python syntax:

Variables:

Introduce the idea that information can be stored using variables.
python
Duplicate code

```
name = "Python"
age = 10
```

Print Articulation:

Demonstrate how to use the print statement to display information.

Python Print the copied code

```
("Hello, Python!")
```

Data Formats:

Talk about normal information types like numbers, floats, strings, and booleans.
Python Copy Code: "Learning Python is fun!" Price: $5.99
is_learning = Valid
Essential Tasks:

Show straightforward number-crunching tasks.
Python's copy code yields 5 plus 3 user input:

Introduce the input function to solicit input from users.
user_name = input("Enter your name:") in the Python copy code
These fundamental ideas give kids the structure blocks to begin coding and exploring different avenues regarding Python. To see the

immediate effects of their changes, encourage them to investigate and alter these examples.

2. Games for Beginners in Python:

2.1 Guess the Number Game

Objective:

Make a game in which the player must guess a number that the computer chooses at random.

Essential Design:

Python's Copy Code imports guess_the_number() from random def:

"Welcome to Guess the Number Game!" is printed.

While True, secret_number = random.randint(1, 100).

surmise = int(input("Enter your conjecture (1-100): "))

if secret_number = guess:
    print("Congratulations! You speculated the right number.")

```
        break
    elif surmise < secret_number:
        "Too low! ", print( Try once
more.
    else:
        print("Too    high!    Attempt
once more.")
```

```
# Uncomment the line beneath to
play the game
# guess_the_number()
```

2.2 Spasm Tac-Toe

Objective:

Create a Tic-Tac-Toe game for two players.

Essential Construction:

Python's copy code has a def print_board(board):

```
  for a board row:
    print(" ".join(row))
```

```
def check_winner(board, player):
   # Look for winning rows,
columns, and diagonals #... def
tic_tac_toe():
   current_player = "X"

   while Valid:
     row = int(input("Enter the row
(0-2):")) in print_board(board)
     col = int(input("Enter the
section (0-2): "))
```

Check to see if the selected cell is empty; if not, ask the player to choose again; update the board and look for a winner; toggle players (X to O, O to X); uncomment the line below to play the game; tic_tac_toe() 2.3 The Goal of Rock, Paper, Scissors

Execute an exemplary Stone, Paper, Scissors game.

14

Fundamental Construction:

```
rock_paper_scissors():     import
random def from python copy code:
   "Welcome   to   Rock,   Paper,
Scissors!" is printed.
   decisions  =  ["rock",  "paper",
"scissors"]

   while Valid:
      user_choice  =  input("Choose
scissors, rock, or paper:") .lower()
      computer_choice            =
random.choice(choices)

      # Contrast user_choice and
computer_choice with decide the
victor
      # ...

# Uncomment the line beneath to
play the game
# rock_paper_scissors()
```

2.4 Executioner

Objective:

Make a straightforward Executioner game where the player surmises a word.

Fundamental Design:

Python's Copy Code imports a random def and uses choose_word():

```
    words           =           ["python,"
"programming,"    "coding,"    and
"challenge"]                    return
random.choice(words),
display_word(word,
guessed_letters), and so on:
    # Show the word with highlights
for unguessed letters
    # ...

def executioner():
    print("Welcome to Executioner!")
    guessed_letters = [] attempts = 6
while attempts > 0: secret_word =
choose_word()
        guess = input("Enter a letter:")
display_word(secret_word,
guessed_letters) .lower()
```

```
    # Check assuming the letter is
in the word
    # Update guessed_letters and
endeavors appropriately
    # ...

    # Check assuming the player
has speculated the whole word
    # ...

# Uncomment the line underneath
to play the game
# executioner()
```

3.1   Drawing   with   Turtle Illustrations

3.1.1   Prologue   to   Turtle Illustrations

What is Turtle Illustrations?

Basic instructions for setting up the Turtle module: forward, in reverse, left, right, penup, pendown

Drawing straightforward shapes: squares, triangles, circles

3.1.2   Turtle   Craftsmanship Activities

Drawing a house

Making mathematical examples

Planning a blossom garden

3.1.3 Test: 3.2 Simple GUI with Tkinter 3.2.1 Getting Started with Tkinter Introduction to Tkinter library Creating a basic window Adding labels, buttons, and entry widgets 3.2.2 Interactive Message Box Displaying information and getting user input Creating a pop-up message box Handling user responses 3.2.3 Building a To-Do List App Designing a simple to-do list interface Adding functionality to add and remove tasks Saving tasks to a file 3.3 Creating a Calculator 3.3.1 Setting Up.

4. Introduction to Information Designs

Information structures, which help us organize and store information in our projects, are similar to compartments. In Python, how about we take a gander at a few tomfoolery and helpful information structures!

4.1.1 What is a Rundown?

4.1 Lists and Arrays A list is a collection of things that can be of a variety of kinds, like numbers, strings, or a wide range of records. Lists are excellent for data storage and organization.

4.1.2 Record-Keeping:

Python Duplicate Code # An illustration of a list of natural products = "apple," "banana," "orange," and "grape" # Getting to the parts of a list print(fruits[0]) # Result: apple" 4.1.3 Changing or Adding to Lists:

```python
Copy code
# Adding a part to the summary
fruits.append("kiwi")

# Wiping out a part from the overview
fruits.remove("banana")

# Reviving a part in the summary
fruits[2] = "pear"
```

4.1.4 Summary Exercises:

```python
Copy Code
# Determine whether an item is in the list
is_apple_present = "apple" in fruits
# Determine the length of the list
num_fruits = len(fruits) # 4.2
```

Dictionaries 4.2.1 What Is a Dictionary?

A word reference is similar to a real word reference, but it applies to your program. It stores data in key-value pairs, which makes it easy to search for and retrieve data.

4.2.2 Referencing Words:

Python Copy code # "name" is an illustration of a person in the dictionary. Alice", "age": 10, "city": " Wonderland" # Obtaining values from a dictionary print(person["name") # Output: Alice" 4.2.3 Editing Dictionary Terms:

Python Duplicate Code # Adding another key-esteem pair person["gender"] = "female" # Eliminating a key-esteem pair del person["age"] # Refreshing the value of a key person["name"] = "Alicia"

Python duplicate code # Counting the quantity of key-esteem matches # Confirming whether a key is in the word reference # Is_age_present = "mature" face to face # Sets 4.3.1 What is a Set?
An extraordinary assortment of parts is known as a set. It is useful when you want to store multiple items while only keeping track of individual values.

4.3.2 Putting Together Sets:

"Red," "Blue," "Green," and "Red" are examples of a set of colors in Python Copy Code. Note: red" will only be taken into account once. 4.3.3 Set Procedures: Number

Tracking down the quantity of components in a set num_colors = len(colors) # It is in the set to Check if a component is_yellow_present = "yellow" in colors # Adding an element to a set of colors.add("yellow") # Removing an element from a set of colors.remove("blue") Python Duplicate code #

5.1 Restrictive Articulations (if, else)

Prologue to Navigation:

explanation of how a program makes decisions.

Statements of If:

Essential sentence structure and use.

Simple illustrations of decisions made every day.

Other assertions:

recognizing potential outcomes.

Guides to build up the idea.

Statements with an if-then clause:

Prologue to settled conditions.

activities for practicing nested logic.

5.2 For and while loops:

Recognizing Repetition:

Clarification of why circles are fundamental for rehashing assignments.

Using Loops:

For loop syntax and usage.

traversing ranges and sequences iteratively.

While Circles:

Utilization of while loops and syntax.

Controlling circle execution with conditions.

Control Statements for the Loop (Break, Continue):

Presenting break and go on for better control.

Examples to show how they are used.

5.3 Functions A Brief Overview of Functions:

justification for the use of functions.

Characterizing Capabilities:

Punctuation for characterizing capabilities.

Making basic capabilities with boundaries.

Calling Capabilities:

how to call functions in various program components.

Passing contentions to capabilities.

Bring Articulations back:

Recognizing the return declaration

Illustrations of functions that return values

Extent of Factors:

elucidating both global and local variables.

The significance of variable extension.

6.1 An Overview of a Text-Based Adventure Game:

Acquaint messes with essential programming ideas through a tomfoolery and intuitive message based experience game.

Key Ideas Covered:

User-Input Steps: Variables, Conditional Statements (if, else), Loops (while), and

Make a storyline with various turning points.

Utilize input articulations to get client decisions.

Carry out restrictive explanations to decide the result.

Use circles to take into account investigation and stretching storylines.

6.2 Overview of the Mini Web Scraping Project:

Introduce youngsters to web scraping in a controlled and instructive setting.

Key Ideas Covered:

Steps for Basic Data Extraction Using HTML:

Select a straightforward website with a simple HTML structure.

To obtain the HTML, make use of the requests library.

To get specific information, make use of a parsing library like BeautifulSoup, for instance.

Show the removed information or save it to a document.

6.3 Overview of Creating a Simple Chatbot:

Connect with kids in making an essential chatbot that answers client inputs.

Key Ideas Covered:

Lists, randomization, and user interaction steps:

Define the purposes of various responses, such as greetings, jokes, and facts.

Utilize a rundown to store potential reactions.

Choose a response at random from the list for each user input.

Set up a loop so that the user can continue to interact with the system until they decide to exit.

7. Cooperative Coding for Youngsters

7.1 Prologue to Form Control with Git

7.1.1 What is Adaptation Control?

Understanding the requirement for variant control in coding projects.
An overview of Git and its role in change tracking.

7.1.2 Essential Git Orders for Youngsters

git init, git add, git commit
Straightforward clarifications and involved activities to build up the orders.

7.1.3 Making a Cooperative Store

Setting up a store on stages like GitHub.

inviting collaborators and describing the workflow for collaboration.

7.1.4 Spreading and Converging for Youngsters

Fundamental ideas of stretching and converging in a youngster cordial way.

Exercises in visualization to assist in comprehending the pattern of change.

7.1.5 Resolving Simple Conflicts An Overview of Conflicts and How to Use Visual Aids to Resolve Them

Using role-playing scenarios to engage in conflict resolution

7.2 Pair Programming Activities

7.2.1 What is Pair Programming?

The advantages and definition of pair programming.

putting an emphasis on teamwork, communication, and solving problems.

7.2.2 Pair Programming for Kids: The Navigator and Driver roles are explained using metaphors that are relatable.

Turning jobs during activities to encounter the two points of view.

7.2.3 Straightforward Pair Programming Difficulties

Coding difficulties intended for matches to tackle together.

promoting discussion and creative thinking.

7.2.4 Constructing a Collaborative Project A guided project in which students collaborate to create a brief program in pairs.

emphasis on sharing and communicating ideas.

7.2.5 Reflecting on the Pair Programming Experience

Discussions among the group about what was successful and what could be improved

Empowering positive input and productive analysis.

7.3 Cooperative Coding Assets

7.3.1 Internet based Stages for Cooperative Coding

Suggesting kid-accommodating stages for cooperative coding projects.

highlighting concerns about privacy and safety.

7.3.2 Coding Games for Joint effort

Presenting coding games that advance cooperation and joint effort.

promoting kid-friendly coding competitions.

7.4.1 Facilitating Collaboration Strategies for educators and parents to foster a collaborative coding environment 7.4 Collaborative Coding Tips

Offsetting individual learning with bunch projects.

7.4.2 Guidelines for Monitoring Online Interactions Online Safety During Cooperative Coding Activities

Open correspondence channels with kids about their encounters.

8.1 Code.org's Kids' Python Online Courses (https://code.org/):

On Code.org, there are numerous kid-friendly free coding courses. They offer courses with notable characters like Minecraft and Frozen and use block-based coding.

Scratch for Kids Programming (https://scratch.mit.edu/): Scratch, a visual programming language and online community, allows children to create and share interactive stories, games, and animations.

The Khan Foundation's Guide to JS: Drawing and Computer Programming (https://www.khanacademy.org/computing): JavaScript can be an extraordinary following stage for youngsters who need to move past block-based coding with the intelligent examples presented by Khan Institute.

CodeCombat (https://codecombat.com/):
Figuring out how to code turns into an undertaking with CodeCombat. Genuine Python and JavaScript code is composed by children, and they can perceive how their characters respond progressively.

8.2 Books that Children Ought to Peruse to Learn Python "Python for Youngsters:

"A Playful Introduction to Programming" by Jason R. Briggs: This book makes Python programming accessible to novices by presenting it in an open and absurd manner.

"Howdy World!: "Computer Programming for Kids and Other Beginners" by Warren and Carter Sande: This book teaches programming concepts through engaging activities and examples using Python.

"Coding Games in Python" by DK: This book gives an involved way to deal with learning Python by consolidating coding practices with the formation of clear games.

8.3 Young Coders' Challenges and Rivals

CoderDojo Individualized Structure Series (https://kata.coderdojo.com/): Children can practice and upgrade their abilities to code with the assistance of the coding difficulties (katas) presented by CoderDojo.

Google Code-in (https://codein.withgoogle.com/): Google Code-in is an annual coding competition for students aged 13 to 17 years old. Participant participation in real-world projects is made possible by open source organizations.

http://www.firstinspires.org/adva nced mechanics/flljr: The First Lego Association Jr. FLL Jr. is a robotics program for young children that teaches STEM concepts and coding through the use of LEGO Education WeDo kits.

CodeCombat Multiplayer Coding Challenges (https://codecombat.com/play): In CodeCombat's multiplayer coding challenges, kids can compete against one another in real-time coding battles.

9.1 Creating an Environment for Supportive Coding:

Create a Dedicated Coding Space in 9.1.1:

Create a dedicated area for coding activities with a comfy chair, good lighting, and few other things going on.

9.1.2 Give the Right Devices:

Guarantee that the youngster approaches a reasonable PC or gadget with the vital programming introduced. Additionally, a dependable internet connection is essential.

9.1.3 Honor Achievement:

To boost the child's confidence, acknowledge and celebrate the smallest accomplishments. To demonstrate their progress, display their projects or accomplishments.

9.1.4 Cultivate a Development Mentality:

Energize an uplifting outlook toward difficulties and missteps. Make it clear that making mistakes is a normal part of learning to code and that learning to code is a journey.

9.1.5 Be a Coding Good example:

Learn the fundamentals of coding yourself if you can. This allows you to participate in your child's learning journey and sets a positive example.

9.1.6 Encourage Teamwork:

Give your child chances to work on coding projects with other kids or siblings. The learning experience can be enhanced by teamwork.

9.2 Adjusting Screen Time:

9.2.1 Specify the Coding Time:

To ensure a healthy balance between screen time and other activities, allocate specific time slots for coding activities.

9.2.2 Integrate Breaks:

Plan customary breaks during coding meetings to forestall eye strain and advance active work. Encourage movement-based activities.

9.2.3 Extend Your Interests:

To provide a well-rounded experience, combine coding with other non-screen activities like reading, outdoor play, or hands-on projects.

9.2.4 Monitoring Data:

Know about the internet based content your kid is drawing in with. Make sure that the tools and platforms for coding are safe and appropriate for children.

9.2.5 Express Expectations:

Expectations regarding screen time limits and the significance of balancing various activities for overall well-being should be clearly communicated.

9.3 Promoting Problem-Solving and Creativity:

9.3.1 Stress Undertaking Based Learning:

Empower the finishing of little coding projects that consider imaginative articulation and critical thinking.

9.3.2 Encourage Curiousness:

Encourage questions and exploration to cultivate a curious mindset. Help children discover solutions and answers on their own.

9.3.3 Include Applications from the Real World:

Interface coding exercises to true applications to show the useful ramifications of their learning.

9.3.4 Present a Variety of Models:

Tell the stories of a variety of people who have used coding to solve problems in the real world. This can motivate inventiveness and expand points of view.

9.3.5 Give Unconditional Difficulties:

Present coding difficulties that have various arrangements. This encourages creative problem-solving and fosters critical thinking.

10.1 Observing Accomplishments

As your young coder finishes Python games and exercises, praising their accomplishments, both of all shapes and sizes is fundamental. Perceiving their advancement supports certainty and inspiration. Consider the following celebration strategies:

Authentications of Accomplishment: Make certificates that are unique and highlight specific achievements. completing a project, mastering a concept, or finishing a game, for instance.

Grandstand Ventures: Kids can show off their favorite projects to parents, friends, or classmates at a mini "Demo Day." This forms certainty as well as urges them to make sense of their code.

Virtual Coding Club: Set up a virtual coding club where kids can talk about their successes, failures, and experiences. This cultivates a feeling of local area and cooperation.

Problems with Coding: Within the group, organize friendly coding challenges. Give small prizes or certificates to the winners to emphasize the fun and collaborative aspects of coding.

10.2 Following stages in Python Learning

In the wake of finishing the underlying arrangement of Python games and exercises, guide kids toward the following stages in their coding process. Provide resources and recommendations for additional research:

Halfway Python Ideas: Introduce concepts like classes and object-oriented programming, which are more advanced. Provide projects that allow students to put these ideas into practice.

Investigate Particular Libraries: Encourage youngsters to investigate Python libraries designed for particular interests. For instance, Beautiful Soup for web scraping, Matplotlib for data visualization, and Pygame for game development.

Project-Based Learning: Make it clear how important it is to learn by doing. Urge them to leave on bigger, more intricate ventures that line up with their inclinations. This could be making a customized site, fostering a more unpredictable game, or robotizing regular errands.

Coding Platforms Online: Investigate online stages that offer intelligent difficulties and coding rivalries. For continuous learning, websites like CodeCombat, Scratch, and HackerRank provide a dynamic environment.

Workshops or camps in coding: Check out kid-friendly coding camps and workshops in your area or online. These projects frequently give organized learning ways, master direction, and open doors for cooperation.

Contributions from Open Source: Present the idea of open source and urge children to add to amateur amicable tasks. This improves their coding abilities as well as imparts a feeling of local area and commitment.